No One Bears Witness for the Witness

BARUCH COHEN

# No One Bears Witness
# for the Witness

a memoir

JOYCE RAPPAPORT
editor

RVP Press New York
CIJR Montreal

**RVP Publishers**

RVP Publishers Inc.
41 East 11th Street, 11th Floor
New York, NY 10003

© 2018 Baruch Cohen / RVP Publishers Inc., New York

The publication of this book was supported by International Center for Western Values, Amsterdam in conjunction with the Canadian Institute for Jewish Research, Montreal.

RVP Press™ is an imprint of RVP Publishers Inc., New York.
The RVP Publishers logo is a registered trademark of RVP Publishers Inc., New York.

Library of Congress Control Number: 2018938053

ISBN 978 1 61861 315 8

www.rvppress.com

# Table of Contents

# *Preface*

*Frederick Krantz*

"No one bears witness for the witness," my colleague, friend and teacher Baruch Cohen often says, quoting his beloved Romanian-Jewish countryman, the great Holocaust poet Paul Celan. This aphorism, which expresses the authenticity which issues only from a person's lived experience, is emblematic of how Baruch has comported himself throughout his long and eventful life (he recently turned an active 98), a life which parallels much of the history of the twentieth, and now the twenty-first, century.

Born in Bucharest, Romania after World War I to a poor Jewish family, exposed to the virulence of pre-World War II Romanian antisemitism, reinforced by the rise of Nazism in Germany and Hitler's accession to power in 1933, Baruch experienced directly the advent of fascist antisemitism in what he terms the Bucharest "Night of Broken Glass" in January, 1941. Searching for his missing father among the bodies of murdered Jews hung on meat-hooks in a Bucharest slaughterhouse (he in fact had survived the pogrom), impressed into forced labor in a work-camp, aware of and evading the death-camps set up in occupied Transnistria, Baruch survived the Holocaust. He married the love of his life, Sonia, with him today, had a beautiful daughter, Monica (Malca), and managed eventually, in 1950, to escape the Communist regime imposed on Romania with the defeat of Germany.

Escape meant beginning a new, and—given the conditions of the time—initially hard life, in recently-reborn Israel. Already a Zionist activist, who had mastered Hebrew before his emigration, Baruch forged new bonds in Israel, working hard, getting business experience, serving in the IDF Reserve during the 1956 Suez-Sinai war, making a warm and loving home with Sonia for Malca. When Sonia's mother and sisters moved to Montreal in 1959, in far-away Canada, and his wife pined for her family, Baruch once again pulled up stakes, and together they left their beloved Israel for a strange New World.

Baruch would flourish in Canada, rising to become head accountant for a major Canadian corporation, and immersing himself in the Jewish community, including the then-new Montreal Holocaust Memorial Centre established by the Jewish Federation. Becoming one of its premier docents, a specialist in communicating the realities of the Holocaust to young high-school and university students, Baruch in the 1970s realized that even the Jewish world knew little of the Holocaust in Romania and Transnistria. Hence much of his life before and after retiring from business was devoted to correcting this historical amnesia, and restoring the memory of the circa 400,000 Jews murdered at the hands of the Romanian fascists and Nazis. As a result of his persistent work, supported by a small group of like-minded persons in Montreal and Toronto, today both the Holocaust museums and research centers in Jerusalem (Yad Vashem) and Washington, D.C., as well as other institutions, feature displays and information on Romania and Transnistria, and the Montreal community now holds an ongoing, annual Romanian Holocaust Commemoration Day, instituted by Baruch Cohen.

Upon retiring in 1988, Baruch decided to do graduate work in Jewish history, taking an M.A. in Jewish Studies at Concordia University. We met in the same year, as the first Palestinian "intifada" terrorist attacks on Israel had begun, and I (a professor of European intellectual history at Concordia) had gotten together a small group of academics and informed laymen which was writing articles and giving talks to rally the community and larger public against the negative and delegitimizing propaganda which had suddenly overwhelmed the media. (This was the period of the invention of the "Holocaust inversion"—still alive in contemporary "BDS" campus anti-Zionism—which claimed that the Palestinians were innocent and impotent "Jews" being oppressed by a powerful, Nazi-like Israel.)

I had noticed some very good "Letters to the Editor" written by one Baruch Cohen, and was about to call him when, serendipitously, we met accidentally on the bus one day. I invited him to join our pro-Israel "ginger group," which he did, and it would be out of this initial group of six or so persons (which began to be invited to give synagogue and study-group talks, and published a continuing series of letters and articles in Montreal and other media) that what was later incorporated as a non-profit research center, the Canadian Institute for Jewish Research, emerged in 1988.

Thus began, for me, a personal friendship and intellectual partnership which has lasted now for thirty years. Baruch brought to the new Institute his experience as a Holocaust survivor, his deep and broad Jewish learning, existential as well as academic, his heartfelt yiddishkayt and commitment to Zionism and the State of Israel, and—not least for a young and inexperienced institution—his concrete, practical business experience and knowledge. And something more—a personal decency, honesty, and sweetness, combined with a quiet persistence and, when necessary, toughness (an "iron fist in a velvet glove," as I came to think of him), which has stood us in good stead across the years, in the face of both political crises and periods of fiscal difficulty.

Baruch became CIJR's Research Chairman, helping to plan our seminar and conferences, working to build our Israel and M.E. Research Databank and Library, overseeing our burgeoning print and electronic publications, and actively training the many student interns who have, across the years, worked at the Institute. As a group largely of academics, it was natural for us to make working with students a key aspect of CIJR's activism—today CIJR boasts the Cohen Summer Israel Intern Fund, established in his name, and as a result of which many of our young pro-Israel community leaders have emerged.

CIJR would not, could not have been the internationally-respected force for intelligent pro-Israel activism which it is today without Baruch Cohen's creative involvement and steady hand. He has been for me a friend and mentor, both a moral and an intellectual support, a teacher in a sense caught by the old German academic term for one's advanced research-degree director, a *Dissertationsvater*, one's dissertation "father," who both teaches and sustains.

One story about him and his impact will suffice for this short introduction. Baruch at CIJR, as in his Holocaust memorial activism generally, made recalling and documenting the Holocaust in still-often-antisemitic Romania a constant theme of his work. We regularly published his articles, which were often picked up and reproduced elsewhere, not least in Jewish (and non-Jewish) publications in contemporary Romania. One day the Israeli ambassador to Canada called, to "congratulate" Baruch—Baruch asked why, and the ambassador told him, "Because you are having such a great impact against antisemitism in Romania that the Romanian ambassador called me personally to plead 'that I call that awful Baruch Cohen and demand that he stop his unfounded attacks at once!'" And before Baruch could reply, the ambassador, laughing, thanked him, and told him to keep up his wonderful work.

Every day for thirty years, Baruch Cohen, witness and survivor, has been a key part of the Canadian Institute for Jewish Research, and part therefore of my life as well. Today, when I greet him at the office, "How are you, Baruch," he smilingly replies, "I am here!" May he be here for many more years, doing what he does so well, defending Israel and the Jewish people, teaching us all through his wide learning and living example, and inspiring our young people and students through his Jewish wisdom, courage, and perseverance.

Finally, this book has been a labor of love and devotion, a tribute from Baruch's academic associates, students, friends and readers. And, as both the fine "Introduction" by Dr. Joyce Rappaport, the volume's able editor, and the latter part of the text itself, will testify, Baruch is not only a Jewish writer and witness of clear political and historical insight and power, but also a talented and moving poet. One of the great pleasures of our work together has been the opportunity to read, and to publish, Baruch's poetry. It is in his poetry that his great love for the Jewish people, and for its eternal capital, Jerusalem, shines most clearly through, and it is here, too, that he has coped with the tragic, premature loss of his and Sonia's beloved and talented Monica/Malca, to whom his poems are often dedicated.

In this regard, allow me to close by citing from one of his most moving poems, "Jerusalem":

> Jerusalem, the city of
> Psalms, tears and joy.
> O! Jerusalem, embraced forever
> With thy people's love!
> O! Jerusalem, a jewel
> Lingering in our hearts!

I bring praise to you, Zion
And thanks forever and ever.
Because I live with eternal
Love for you!

―――――――――――――

*Dr. Frederick Krantz, Director of the Canadian Institute for Jewish Research, is Professor of History at Liberal Arts College, Concordia University, Montreal.*

# Introduction

*Joyce Rappaport*

The book that you are holding is a most precious gift—the memoir of Baruch Cohen. This is a work of historical significance, far beyond a personal autobiography. Baruch wrote his story and dedicated it to his wife Sonia and his grandchildren and great-grandchildren. They will love to read about his life in Bucharest, Israel, and Montreal, and will learn from it. And they will see a side of a young Baruch, whom perhaps they could not imagine, a young boy who loved pets and horses, and sports, and going to the cinema, and helping his parents around the home.

But we, his audience, from Montreal, from the Canadian Institute for Jewish Research, from the Holocaust Centre in Montreal, from the students with whom he interacted, Jewish and non-Jewish, will find other lessons that Baruch continues to teach us, written in stark images that we will not forget. Baruch tells us about growing up, poor though not deprived, in a neighbourhood in Bucharest, where Jews and non-Jews alike lived in relative harmony. His words give us the sense of the life of a young boy and adolescent, attending school, being part of Jewish youth groups, relating to his parents and sisters, but then suddenly seeing the Jewish world come crashing down. Baruch's own mother expressed it in no uncertain terms, when in 1933 Hitler came to power, and she said to her son, "Baruch, this is the end of the Jewish people." She was sharp enough to know that their life in Europe was going to end.

It did not end entirely, though. Baruch lived through the Holocaust, suffering through beatings and chilling experiences in forced-labour work camps. The memoir contains details that he has not talked about. He survived and helped his family through bitter suffering. During the darkest days of the war, he never gave up his goodness. He fell in love and married Sonia, who dedicated her life to him, and supported him in all his creative endeavours and in his passion to tell the truth about anti-semitism. They became the parents of Monica, and moved to Israel and then to Canada to live a full and safe Jewish life. But it was a life tinged with sadness even in their later years, for the hardest tragedy of all was when Monica passed away in 2000. And yet his own resilience did not fade—so strong was his need to teach and share his message.

Baruch continues patiently to teach us. He made it his life commitment to let the world know the atrocities of the Romanian Antonescu regime. Here in Canada he has taught us about the Romanian Jewish experience—he was foremost in exposing Canadian reading audiences to the poetry of Paul Celan, whom Baruch knew in Bucharest, and to whom he bade farewell when Celan left Romania. Baruch also exposed the horrors of the Holocaust in Transnistria, where thousands of Jews were deported and killed, placing Transnistria on the map when no one else had heard of the massacres and slaughters that occurred there. He tirelessly organized yearly Transnistria commemorations, giving a voice to the silent murdered Jewish victims. Recently, Baruch passed the baton to the younger generation to make sure that those victims will never be forgotten.

Baruch is modest and was not pleased when a number of us tried to convince him to write his story. But Professor Frederick Krantz, director of the Canadian Institute for Jewish Research, Lenore Krantz, and others at the Institute pleaded with him to do so—if only just for his family. Baruch, today at age 98, still serves as Research Director at the Institute, continuing to give the perspective of a one who was "there," both in the grim times in Eastern Europe and in happier years in Israel.

When Baruch (most reluctantly!) began to write his story, he worked especially with two people who were student editors at the time, Jacqueline Leebosh and David Anidjar. Together at CIJR we transcribed recordings that Baruch had made at the Montreal Holocaust Memorial Centre and interviewed Baruch to expand his details. Without Jacqueline and David, this book would never have been completed.

The memoir also contains some works of true passion and beauty: Baruch's poetry. A section with some thirty poems, published over the years in CIJR's *Isranet* and *Israfax* journals, tells us of his anguish over his life's events, both personal and cultural, and conveys his love of Jewish history, of Israel and of Jewishness. They, too, are a worthy vision of a Jewish life in troubled times, and part of Baruch Cohen's legacy to us.

─────────────

*Dr. Joyce Rappaport served as a research associate at the Canadian Institute for Jewish Research from 1998 to 2004. She currently is the executive editor of the Posen Library of Jewish Culture and Civilization, a 10-volume anthology series published by Yale University Press.*

# Part I

Romania, 1942

source: U.S. Holocaust Memorial Museum

# *Childhood*

This memoir is written for my family—for my two grandsons Mark and Stuart, for their wives Sara and Emily, and for my beloved great-grandchildren. Through my words, they will learn about a Jewish past in a country and culture that no longer exists. They will learn about my childhood and young years in pre- and post-Holocaust Romania, and will discover how my experiences were haunted by the disease of anti-Semitism, and how I learned its lessons and have strived to pass them on. They will read about my struggles and my joys, and about my dear wife Sonia, and her story, too. They will read about our beloved daughter, Malca, who made their own lives possible, and who, too, survives in these words.

As I write these words, I am 98 years old, and feeling the years. Nonetheless, I look back and can recall so much about my childhood in the city of Bucharest, Romania, where I was born on October 15, 1919. As I write my story, I see myself, my parents, and my three sisters in our small house on 76 Vulturilor Street. We were poor, we were needy, but we still lived in a private home surrounded by a yard with two trees and their fruits.

The Cohen family, Bucharest, 1923
Baruch, his parents and sisters

My father, Mordecai Cohen, was born in the 1880s, and came from the town of Hertza in Moldava, northern Romania. His early years are a mystery to me; we never visited his town, and I don't even know how far away it was from us by train. Mordecai himself seemed to be a man alone in the world—I never knew anyone from his family, not my grandparents, not his brothers or sisters. Indeed, I don't even know if he had any siblings. He did not talk about his family, and I did not think to ask.

My father was a simple man, an uneducated man. Surely, one asks, he must have been able to read. But I can state without doubt that he had no education, none at all. He did his work, and cared about supporting his wife and children. But intellectually, he was not a sophisticated man. He worked at manual jobs, doing anything that he could find as a day labourer. His life was a struggle. At one point he wanted to set up a small stand in the streets of Bucharest, selling items such as shoelaces. However, he lacked the business sense to handle even such a small enterprise. Sometimes if he had money, he would try to set up a table for himself, but usually he would take any job that he could find, working in shops, helping salesmen, helping put together orders. He helped in shops, not fields (we were in a large city), and not at factories.

My father was totally illiterate. I discovered this when I was in about grade four. It was a Sunday and he was home, and I was working on my homework. He asked to see what I was doing, and to my dismay I noticed that he held my book upside down. Many years later, when I was in my late twenties, I attempted to teach him to write his name, but unfortunately I did not succeed. Without diminishing my respect for him, for he was a kind man whose family was important to him, I still must stay that he had no interests at all, none at all. He had no friends. He was a fine human being, one who would never insult another. But he was a loner. It hurts me to say that he was so void of interests.

We had a big yard and my older sister liked small animals. One day my father came home in the evening and a little dog was missing. My father was so upset that we walked around Bucharest until early in the morning, finally finding the little dog. This is something that I never have forgotten, and it shows a sympathetic side of my dear father.

The only part of his life that he alluded to was his military experience during World War I. I knew this from him. As a soldier in the Romanian army, he came home having earned a small medal. He gave me this medal, but never told me what it was for. Had he been in a battle? Was he awarded it for his bravery? Again, as with other parts of his life, he never talked about it. I no longer have the medal—it was something that I had to leave behind when I emigrated.

Nor was my father religious: not at all. But like so many Jews of that time, he went to *shul* on Shabbat, unless he had to work. And of course he attended synagogue on Rosh Hashanah and Yom Kippur. Why did he do this? That's the way it was in the Jewish communities of Eastern Europe. He went because he knew he was a Jew; other Jews went to synagogue, so he did too. He must have grown up with these traditions because he knew how to pray even if he did not know the meanings of the chants. He also came to synagogue because of my mother.

In contrast to my father, my mother was literate, educated, and intelligent. Her name was Fannie Hershkowitz—Fayge in Yiddish and Tzipora in Hebrew. A few years younger than my father, she was born in Brăila, a city close to the Danube River north of Bucharest. She had completed four grades of school, and despite not continuing her formal education she wrote well, read the Romanian and Yiddish newspapers, and listened to the radio, following the news. A highlight of her day was reading the papers; sellers came from home to home, or she would borrow the newspaper from a neighbour. She also wrote beautifully, and it was she who inspired my own love of writing. In my fondest memories, I see her sitting on a chair, reading in our beautiful yard. She was kind and astute, and well aware of the significance of world events. In 1933 when Hitler came to power, she said to me, "Baruch, this is the end of the Jewish people." She was sharp enough to know.

Mother stayed at home, like most Jewish women, and she cooked, cleaned, and took care of her children. Like my father, she was not religious, but she still baked challahs, lit candles on Friday night, prepared a sumptuous meal, and could follow prayers in the *siddur*. Although we could not afford to join a synagogue, from time to time she went to services on Saturdays.

I had three sisters, two older and one younger. Chaya was the eldest, some four or five years older than I was, and then came Sarah, about two years later. After I was born, my mother gave birth to Golda, who was two or three years younger. Later in life, Chaya married a cousin.

Sarah, a very beautiful girl, was not lucky in her life. She met a handsome Hungarian Jew who did not have a trade. Still, she loved him and they got married. Then, however, he got sick, and passed away, and she never remarried. After the war she lived in Israel.

In our home, we never went to sleep without eating; we were never hungry. We were always cleaned and dressed properly. I slept in my parents' room and my sisters had their own room. Our house did not have a bathroom, and my sisters often complained about this inconvenience.

At home, we spoke Romanian. My parents talked to each other in Yiddish, but my mother insisted that we know Romanian well. There was such terrible anti-Semitism that she was afraid that if we spoke Yiddish, we would be mocked. My mother also did not want us to look "too Jewish"; therefore, my father was clean-shaven, and I did not wear a kippa.

Our house was on a typical lower-middle-class street in Bucharest. As I mentioned, we had a large yard, as well as a kitchen, two bedrooms, and a third room that my parents rented out to people, including to my mother's brother Iancu until he married. The rent money was very helpful. It was an apartment with a big back yard. The owner was a Romanian Christian who would come around to collect the rent. I remember one day he remarked to my mother, "Mme Cohen, how can you manage to bring up four children?" He knew that my father hardly could make a living. But we could always pay the rent, and we always had our Friday night Shabbat dinners, with our father reciting *kiddush*.

Most of the people in our neighbourhood were Jewish, though not Orthodox. We had Christian neighbours and were on good terms with them. Our house was on a clean street, in a section close to the so-called "poor" part of the city. Around 1933, electricity arrived in the district; before that, the streets were lit by old-fashioned gaslight by a man who would come by at dusk. Inside, we heated our home with wood. We were not close to downtown. To get downtown required a 15- to 20-minute walk to the tram. However, we were not far from a main shopping street, where my mother would sometimes go, and there was an adequate grocery store 10–15 minutes closer.

We also lived near several synagogues and a Jewish school that I attended. Of course, with a large Jewish population, there were synagogues all over Bucharest, and some were quite far away—sometimes my parents would walk for at least half an hour to get to one. Their favourite synagogue was in a tall building that accommodated at least two hundred people. Across the street was the prominent Sephardic synagogue. People would also go to services at *shtibls*, small prayer places that met in a home. I loved the architecture of the large synagogue we attended, and like other children on the holidays we would run out of the building, exploring other synagogues as well.

My home was secure, poor but secure and full of love. I didn't wander far from our immediate environment, but the world still opened up to me. Quite early on, I found a mentor and model in my favourite uncle, my mother's younger brother Iancu (Yacov). Uncle Iancu was my window into another kind of life. I loved him very much, and he had faith in my ambitions.

Iancu was literate and learned. Not only had he completed high school, but he finished university as well, getting his accounting degree. He was a successful accountant, and he served as the director of a bank in downtown Bucharest, the Bank of Industry and Commerce. I studied hard, thanks to him. Not only did he teach me to achieve in my school and career, but he gave me my love of *Yiddishkayt*, Hebrew, and literature. Whatever I am today is because of this man.

My mother also had an older brother too, Max Hershkowitz, who was a traveling salesman, who like all of us struggled to make ends meet. He had at least three children and was busy with them. At first, Iancu was not married, and we saw him very often. Eventually he married a lovely Russian woman.

Unlike children today, we had no store-bought toys. But one of my earliest memories was about a tender gift that Iancu gave me. I was about seven years old, and like many boys, especially back then, I loved horses. One day Uncle Iancu dropped by, and was speaking to my mother. All of a sudden he said, "Baruch, come with me, I want to show you something." He opened the door to the yard, and there I saw a little toy horse, made for a child to play. He said, "Go to it. It's a present for you." I was emotional, and still am when I think about it now. This miniature horse was the first present I had ever received. Certainly my father couldn't afford to give me a gift like that. I approached it gingerly and was afraid to touch it. Made of material, it was stuffed and was the most precious gift I have ever had. I will never forget it!

Uncle Iancu also inspired my love of history. From early on, including at school, I wanted to know more about the Jewish people. Why were we persecuted? Iancu encouraged me to learn Biblical history, to learn where we came from. I indulged myself in reading about King Solomon, David, and then the post-Biblical age. As I grew older I learned about Babylon and about Rome. Iancu would bring me books and stories to read. I also loved literature and adventure stories, but could not afford to take books from the library. Sometimes I would get a wealthier friend to borrow a book for me.

Education was a prime value in my family. Unfortunately, my family could not afford to pay for our schooling, and my sisters all left school at age ten. They then worked at sewing dresses, and the money they earned helped to support the family.

I stayed in school as long as I could, first studying at a Jewish Romanian school, called the United Jewish Schools. I mastered Hebrew and learned about Jewish holidays and history. Here again I was fortunate to have my uncle's support. He refused to let me work to help the family, and insisted that I continue studying.

School would start in the morning at 8 or 9 o'clock. There were more than one hundred students there, divided into boys and girls. We did not have to wear a uniform, but I would wear short pants. After four years, when it was time for upper-level education, I attended the Tarbut (Cultura) school, and my uncle paid the tuition. I completed four upper grades, and then had to go to work, even though I longed to go to university.

My childhood was also a time for friendships and simple pleasures. I liked soccer and skating. Even though we didn't have money to buy skates, we would improvise, taking pieces of wood, putting them under our shoes with thread, and running on the ice. Sports interested me, too, and I attended the Jewish Maccabee club. However, I did not have the money to compete. We could not play real soccer, but rolled together a pretend ball, made out of *shmatas*, rags.

I also liked to go to the movies, but it was impossible for us to afford to do so. My mother did manage to put some money aside to go to the Romanian or Jewish theatre.

Across the street, my neighbour Victor was about my age. We played together but his mother was very anti-Semitic and made it difficult for him to play with a Jewish boy. Victor became strongly influenced by his mother, and we drifted apart. We also had two other neighbours: on the right side was a cobbler. On the left side was a Christian family, Romanian of German origin. One of their daughters became a Hitler youth, though the other sister had a Jewish boyfriend. For me, the general atmosphere of anti-Judaism was a factor every day, though I don't remember being beaten by anyone because I was a Jew. There were always taunts in the street.

I tried to be just an ordinary young Jewish boy. I enjoyed being with my friends, and even had some pre-teen crushes on girls. The daughter of one of my teachers was a beautiful young girl named Sidonia. I was just ten but we talked a lot. Her parents were not happy with the idea of their daughter dating a "poor Baruch." I even told my mother about her.

My more carefree days drew to an end as I approached my bar mitzvah celebration. The only people who came to the synagogue were my parents and my uncle. My mother made a little cake; we left most of it at the synagogue. When we came to our home, she asked me bring some cake to our neighbours—and that was my bar mitzvah.

It was the end of 1932. No one could have predicted the next phase of our lives as Europe began its assaults on Jews, leading to the genocide of our people.

* * *

The year 1937 brought radical changes into Romanian politics. There had always been anti-Semitism, but it had not been legislated. In 1937, the government of Goga and Kuza proclaimed racial laws, marking the start of a most bitter time, a reflection of the Nazi years. I remember the anguish, that year or a bit later, when Romanian Jews had their citizenships revoked. It did not matter one iota that my father was a veteran of World War I, who had fought in the Romanian army *for* Romania. We all lost our citizenship. I was then about 18 years old, and was shocked, profoundly. At 18 or 19, I should have been able to join the military service. But now I was abandoned by my country. Though I had experienced anti-Semitism before, I never could have anticipated that it would have gone so far.

As time went on, Nazi Germany had more and more of an influence on Romanian politics. After a year or so—I don't remember the exact day—King Carol was sent away, and his son, King Mihail, took over the rule of the country. He was really just a puppet, and the cruelty truly began when General Antonescu took over. That, for me, meant the beginning of the Holocaust in Romania. At that point, I was working at my Uncle Max's company; he had found me a job there, at the Swiss firm called Richenbacher. He had written a letter of recommendation for me, and it had led to a job.

I began to lose my so-called friends. As I walked home one day, for the first time I confronted the true horror of anti-Semitism. On the sidewalk, I met up with a group of youngsters, "friends" with whom I used to attend movies. They taunted me, saying, *You are a Jew, Yehuda; you have to walk on the other side of the street.* I wasn't a very strong guy, and I always tried to avoid fighting, so I crossed to the other side of the street. After a few moments, the same group of boys teased me, saying, "We told you that you're not allowed to walk on this side." So I replied, "You told me the *other* side," and they laughed back, "No, you have to walk in the middle of the street." That encounter remained with me, and it bothers me even today.

Then we began to hear about pogroms and mass killings in other Romanian cities. The news came from individuals, through word of mouth—not from official reports. And in January 1941, the Holocaust came to Bucharest, my city. For three days and three nights, we experienced what I call the Bucharest *Kristallnacht*, a disaster perpetrated by the Romanian population that shocked the authorities; it was even a surprise to the German army occupying our city. Antonescu, Prime Minister since 1940, put a stop to the destruction after three days. But in that time, the Jews of Bucharest were ruined and we were frightened. Our homes were destroyed, along with our synagogues and our stores. The beautiful Choral Synagogue, so highly respected, was a major victim of the destruction. I have heard that even the German authorities thought that this was not acceptable. The Germans believed that Jews were *supposed* to be deported and killed *somewhere*, but not in the cities, not in full view of the capital of Romania.

On the first day of the Romanian *Kristallnacht*, I was coming home from work, approaching the place where we were living. Standing in the yard in front of our home was a Christian man whose name I still remember, Georgi Dobrescu. He pleaded, "Baruch, quickly go into your house. I already told your mother and your sister to go into your cellar and stay there—I'll stand here in front and will make sure that no one touches you." He was a Christian, and when I talk to students, I am very careful to mention this—that not all Christians participated in acts of barbarism.

This man was a neighbour. We used to send our shoes to him to repair. We had known each other for years, and would play with his children. But it was one of his sons who was amongst the group that mocked me, "You are a Jew, you are not supposed to. . . ." We had played soccer together, but it did not matter in the face of anti-Semitism.

Those things still bother me today. The memories are disturbing and even as I get older and older, they come back to me often, making me extremely upset.

The Bucharest *Kristallnacht* was instigated by a gang of youngsters. My wife, whom I did not yet know, had an uncle who was beaten and whose life and home were destroyed. He was a well-off man who had owned a bakery on one of the main streets. The thugs took him and beat him in such a way that after two or three weeks he needed surgery to amputate both his hands and legs. I still have nightmares and cannot forget this event; even as I get older and older and older, my will to continue suffers at such memories.

I was with my mother and my three sisters. We heard nothing about our father. After the third day, rumours started to spread in the city, and families who were missing loved ones were advised to go to the slaughterhouse, which was located in a beautiful forest outside of Bucharest called the Jilava. People were saying, "Go there, maybe you'll find your brother or . . ." I proceeded there, mentally prepared to find my father dead. He was not there, but I encountered the most shocking image of my life: corpses hanging from meat hooks, with mocking signs attached, "advertising" Jewish meat or Jewish kosher meat.

The signs still haunt my thoughts, with memories of people hanging, like meat in the slaughterhouse. Not many people know about this. Published statistics say that some 130 people were killed at that location. Some of them were lying down—their images were preserved in some books, showing bodies lying covered with sheets. Their relatives arrived and uncovered the sheets to see if their loved ones were there.

Normally this slaughterhouse was used to process beef, but now it held human corpses. I also went to the morgue and the forest and still could not find my father.

During this time of high tension, we remained in the cellar. We had electricity and water, and were able to arrange to get some food from the grocery store across the street, so we did not starve. But my father was still not home, and we could barely hear any news; our house was not on the main street. We gradually discerned that the situation was getting quieter, so along with our neighbours we decided to leave. But my father still had not come home.

He was safe, though we did not know this immediately. He had been working somewhere at the outskirts of Bucharest, very far from our house, and a Christian man said to him, "Mr. Cohen, I won't let you go home because things are dangerous for Jews in the city. We'll give you a piece of bread and find a place for you here." It was only after the fourth day, perhaps the 24th or 25th of January—I cannot vouch for the exact date—he made his way home. He was fine. And he even didn't know what had happened, as he had been hiding in a section of the city where more Christians than Jews lived.

We wanted to get back to our lives, but the fears and scars dominated our moods. My uncle Iancu was a victim. The night my father came home, Iancu was slashed terribly and beaten on the street. We also could not ignore the destruction of Jewish-owned buildings and businesses. We walked outside of our areas, and toward the main streets that were fifteen to twenty minutes away. There we saw Jewish-owned stores, with their windows broken and contents looted. Other places had been set on fire, as I had seen on that first day, when I had been at work. The skies were red from the flames of homes that had been set on fire. Even today I can't sleep well, recalling these images. I also passed the Mareh Synagogue, where my mother used to attend Shabbat services. Its beautiful walls were damaged. Not far away were three or four other synagogues in our Jewish neighbourhood, all of which had been damaged. The Orthodox Chevra Kadisha and the Conservative Brotherhood synagogue suffered. And not far away was a damaged synagogue attended by Hasidic Jews. We were part of a very large Jewish community.

The events of January 1941 were the turning point for me. And what bothers me to this day, is that when I came to Canada and Montreal, I discovered that nobody knew about our suffering. Indeed, people were saying that the Holocaust had not come to Romania. Those comments hurt me, pushing me to write the truth.

After the Bucharest *Kristallnacht*, I went back to work. Mr. Richenbacher, my boss, was called back to Switzerland and his replacement was a German, a bitter man whose hatred for Jews was obvious in his face. He didn't insult me, and did not hurt me physically, but I could see that he didn't like me. And after a while he told me to leave, that it would be better for me to find another job. The atmosphere at the company was tense. Two women I worked with, Heidi and Lina (Caroline) were Christian Germans. One of them was tolerant but the other was quite anti-Semitic. I tried to keep working there, until the following summer, when the firm told me that they didn't need me any longer.

In June 1941, the Germans attacked the Soviet Union, and the war grew more brutal. Even before this, Germans steadily came into Romania. We saw them all around Bucharest. German officers and soldiers walked freely about. We'd encounter them going to movie houses and restaurants. I remember seeing a Romanian actress, a beautiful woman, walking on the main street with a German officer, and they were embracing and kissing. The majority of Romanians were very friendly with the Germans. We did not see a lot of troop action, but nearby, in a city called Ploesh [Ploesti (Wallachia)]—maybe 30 kilometers outside of Bucharest—the German army arrived to take over the town's famous oil refineries.

June 22, 1941 is recalled by most of the world as the day Germany invaded the Soviet Union. We learned about it from our neighbours' reports of radio broadcasts (I didn't catch this news on our small radio). Jews were quite rightfully scared, and many changed their locations, feeling that something was about to happen. Because we had relatives in northern Romania, we tried to find out what was happening, but the news came only by word of mouth. We didn't have a telephone. We were very concerned, but it was quite quiet. I am assuming that some Jews were afraid to talk.

But more shocking to us, in Romania, were the horrors perpetrated in the city of Iaşi on June 28th and 29th. *Thirteen thousand* Jews were killed. And several thousand other Jews were sent away by train in closed cars, wagons without air. At that point, we didn't know the magnitude of numbers, but we were beginning to grasp the horrors that lay ahead. We felt closed in, with nowhere to hide. We could not think of running away or hiding. I, the only son, could not think of abandoning my mother and three sisters. My father was illiterate; he did whatever he could to find work. My sisters had worked from the age of nine. I could not dream of running away.

We, like most other Jews in a country with 800,000 Jews, were so desperate that we couldn't even think about the full extent of the horrors. Some Jews were in denial; others were not so involved with Jewish life and could pretend for a while that they were not affected.

Dismissed from my job, I started to work on the black market, buying household items and selling them for a profit. I bought and sold threads, materials, and dry goods, but not food or cigarettes. My uncle helped me, directing me to underground places where I could find such items. I would bring samples to people, and then search for products to sell, earning a small profit. I had to wrap and carry everything by myself, disguising the merchandise. Once I made a sale, I would get cash immediately, and could buy food, which I would bring home to my mother.

In this way, we avoided starvation. My father did what he could, and my sisters worked at dress places, so we could manage. Perhaps every second week we were able to buy a chicken, and we'd take it to the kosher slaughterer. We tried to keep our Shabbat traditions on Friday night, having a Friday evening supper all together. We still were able to purchase vegetables, because peasants went around the neighbourhood with carts. From time to time we found fruit: apples, cherries, and things that grew locally. I also tried to dress decently, wearing old items from my Uncle Iancu, that my mother would patch up. Never something new.

We tried to maintain our morale. My mother was our motivation, as she followed the news. Our neighbour the cobbler, with whom we had a good relationship, would give her the daily newspapers to read. She was terrified of what was going on in the world. My father was more ignorant; he just lived, ate, went to work, came home, and slept. The stress obviously affected us day by day, though it was not always the same. Shifts in the political situation affected our moods and patterns. When something went wrong for the Romanian army, the stress filtered down to everyone.

In 1941, I was twenty-two years old. I was not confined to our home, and I tried, like any other young man, to have a social life. I did go to the occasional movie, but the theatre was out of the question; it was just too expensive. Instead, I spent most of my time reading, delving into my uncle's great library. I even had a few girlfriends, neighbours and friends of neighbours. But entertainment was limited. We did not dare to go out late at night.

If young men or women socialized or dated, they would walk through the beautiful parks of Bucharest. What would we talk about? I always tried to discuss the books I was reading. Anything else was too dangerous or too costly. It was rare that I would go to a restaurant; dining out was very expensive. Only occasionally, when I had sold some objects or had gotten a small raise, I would eat at a restaurant in a district outside the centre of the city. Away from downtown, one could find middle-class restaurants, not high-end. I would also sometimes indulge in visits to cafés that sold all kinds of sweet things; from time to time I could afford to do that. And it was rare that I drank alcohol, beyond the *Kiddush* wine after my father's prayers on Friday nights and holidays.

By the end of the summer of 1941, thoughts of peace came to an end. The government established forced-labour battalions. Back in June 1941, following the slaughter in Iaşi, I was so-called "invited" to register with the police. As I left the house for my appointment in July, my mother advised, "Take something warm with you, because they might keep you longer than you expect." I replied, "No! I'll come back soon." So I went lightly dressed to the police, joining twenty-four men who were my age. After we had stood for six or eight hours, an officer came out and announced, "Well, we are going to take you away from Bucharest." We asked if we could inform our parents, but the police said no. A group of Romanian soldiers surrounded all twenty-four of us, saying "We'll lead you out of here." And so we started to march along the streets of Bucharest. Some people were indifferent to this spectacle, while others asked the officers what was wrong. They would reply, "They are Jews; we are taking them out of Bucharest." Some of the passersby behaved decently, but others spat at us, crying out, "Kill the Jews, kill them!" We walked for a few hours, leaving Bucharest and coming to a field that was an army headquarters with a soccer field. There the officer ordered us into the middle of the field. Another officer came out and gave one of the most violent, vicious talks against Jews—"You Jews! You are not getting out of this place. This is where you are going to stay." Well, I am here now and I am telling this story. We received no water, and no food. It was already almost 8:00 or 9:00 at night, and one of the officers shouted, "You see those barracks there? That is where you are going to sleep." It was a large, immense place. But with the barracks there was also a horses' stable. Before we could lie down, we were ordered to clean the place. Clean with what, we asked?

So we cleaned. And finally we lay down, but it was already dark and we were starving and tired. And I don't know if it was after one, two, or three hours, but a soldier came over to me like all others and ordered, "Come with me." And I went. He brought me to a cell and started to beat me, with the back of a rifle, until I fainted and fell down. He then threw cold water on me, and when I emerged from the faint, he beat me again—causing my lower spine to break (which ultimately required surgery, in Canada in the 1950s). After a few more hours of brutality, he said, "You go now, but I will call you back."

That same night, two of the twenty-four of us tried to run away, and both of them were shot. There were only twenty-two of us in the morning. At 5:00 AM we finally were given a cup of black tea. No sugar, no food, no bread, just the tea. After twenty-four hours, the officer said he was going to put us to work. We discovered what our jobs were to be: because the war was starting to approach Bucharest, they needed to dig trenches.

The conditions were horrible. At first, the food we were given to eat was corn flour; it was black and in reality was food for animals. After a few days we were given a little bit more food. And as days passed by, more youngsters arrived. They took us out to dig trenches, anti-tank trenches. After a few weeks, I went to work in the morning at 6:00. I wasn't a strong guy, so after a very short time I fainted and fell, and my friend said, "Baruch, stand up because you don't know what will happen or where they will take you or if you'll come back alive or not." But I couldn't stand up, so they carried me on a stretcher.

After about a month, we were told that we would receive visits from our families. And as the families were announced, every parent came with a bag of food or a shirt—for more than a month we had been wearing the same shirt. I remember sitting at a table, watched over by Romanian soldiers. My mother came with my older sister to bring me changes of clothes. After my family left, all the food was taken away. They only let us keep the shirts and pants.

My mother and sister were powerless to do anything after they saw the circumstances under which I was held. What could they do? There were soldiers around, and the soldiers claimed they would give food to me later. I was able to talk to my family for a few moments, and my mother and sister were crying.

I stayed in confinement for several months, until February 1942, digging trenches with a shovel, and I was there with some former classmates. One day, the officer said that we would be going back to Bucharest. None of us believed him, and we dreaded where they might really be taking us. However, in the end we went back to the same place that we had left. After a few hours they told us that we could go free. I couldn't believe it because I was sure that when we turned around they would shoot us. But here I am today.

I was weak, blistered, and hungry. We had subsisted on pieces of hard black bread, which I would soften in the black tea. When they told us that we were free to go home, I arrived, and I walked into the door of my house. My middle sister saw me and fainted. She did not recognize me.

# Part II

Baruch Cohen, 1942

# *War*

In the summer and fall of 1941, we knew that the war was coming closer to Bucharest. We would see groups of military planes—five or ten at once—flying overhead. We weren't sure if they were German or Romanian. Ultimately, we learned that American and British planes were bombing the oil refineries near Bucharest. I had dug trenches from June to the beginning of January/February of 1942.

The forced labour broke my body. I was in weak physical shape when I arrived home and would lie on the sofa, trying to sleep. I was no longer used to sleeping like a human being, and in the middle of the night I would move onto the floor. I was home for just a few weeks, resting and eating a little better, when I was called again to do forced labour, cleaning the streets of snow and sticks.

Soldiers and police brought the work notifications to the forced labourers. We were enumerated on a list and they knew where we lived, and they'd say we had to show up the next morning at a police station. I was afraid I would be sent somewhere again, but this time I came home every evening and could eat and sleep at my place, setting out each morning again. This time, also, I was dressed in an overcoat and wore boots. Nonetheless, Romania is cold in the winter, with very sharp, strong winds.

Several hundred of us would be out in the streets, bunched together in groups of about ten. A guard with a rifle, a soldier, stood over us, telling us what to do. Sometimes we could get him to lessen the workload, by getting him coffee or other items. Wealthier members of our group could even show up in the morning, stay for roll call, pay off the soldier, and leave for the day. I didn't have the money so I had to be there every day.

When spring arrived, we were left alone. Life almost went back to normal, though from day to day they would check identity cards in the city. The relaxed routine turned out to be a very drastic change. Still, I was not allowed to work officially, so I continued to sell things on the black market. My back was still in a lot of pain, and I had no access to medicines. My mother tried to help by wrapping up my back in a towel.

By the summer of 1942, we sensed that the Romanian army was not strong. The Germans, too, were losing their effectiveness. I was at home for most of the summer, not part of the army or in forced labor. But we knew that something was happening. People caught up with the news on the radio and were talking. My father was taking any kind of day labour he could find, and my mother maintained the house. While we certainly were not happy, we were pleased to hear that the Germans were not achieving all of their goals.

In 1943, some of my friends grew interested in Zionism. I was approached by members of a Jewish society to distribute flyers for Zionist organizations. We also followed the news in a paper called the *Jewish Gazette*; it was critical of the government and informative about Jewish situations. My mother admonished me for putting myself into danger, but even she said that she could not stop me from doing what I had to do.

I didn't attend meetings of Zionist organizations, but spent time talking about the Jewish future. We discussed where we would live after the war, assuming we survived. We never planned acts of sabotage, nor were we aware of any outside help coming from the Land of Israel into Romania. Our pamphlets were printed on small pieces of paper that announced that it was time for people to move to *Eretz Israel*. My uncle and my mother were actually very enthusiastic when they heard about *Eretz Israel*. But I still kept my activities low-key. I tried not to make a big splash about it, especially to my mother because she was very concerned that I would get hurt. I distributed pamphlets to Jewish homes. Sometimes at night I would be shoving pamphlets under a door. I always carried some inside my coat, and that in itself was quite dangerous. If I met somebody who was interested in Zionism, I tried to slip the papers to them as secretly as possible.

We also knew that people did try to escape to go to the Land of Israel. That was their sole destination. Through word of mouth of relatives, we were aware of the story of the ship called the *Struma*, which sank in February 1942 near Greece. The *Struma* and another ship, the *Nefkur*, tried to reach the shores of Israel. The *Struma* had more than 700 people aboard, and only one person survived. The *Nefkur* had 360 people. In total, more than 1,000 people were killed. We tried to follow such stories on the radio, but we were terrified that our neighbours would hear us listening.

Other people ran away from Romania by foot, crossing the border into Austria and Germany. My brother-in-law left like that. He was not married then, but he later married my sister-in-law, my wife's sister. I myself was not yet ready to go because I didn't want to leave my parents.

When we heard on the radio that Gen. Friedrich Paulus had surrendered at Stalingrad (February, 1943) we knew that this was a gigantic disaster for Germany, something for us to celebrate. Still, we could not imagine the magnitude of this disaster. The German army was still in

Baruch and Sonia Cohen

Romania, and even though they started to retreat they were still present. Nonetheless, we knew that this crack in their armour marked the beginning of the end.

By summer, 1943 there were still German soldiers in Bucharest, but life was so-called normal in comparison to the way it had been for the past two or three years. My friends and I would get together to dance, talk, and walk. Life seemed a bit less restrictive, unless there were German soldiers around, and they were less present than they had been. I went out with a group of people my age and met a few girls. Among them was my future wife.

Her name was Sonia Lift, and she, too, was from a family in Bucharest. Her father was a tailor, a very successful one. Even at that time, he had wealthy clients, mostly not Jewish. Sonia and her sister were not as affected by the war as we were; they could afford a much better lifestyle than we had.

We fell in love, both of us, right away. And after six months or so, on December 26, 1943, we got married. We married at lunch time, with a ceremony at the synagogue. The rabbi was there, of course, but only a few people attended: my parents, my sisters and her uncle, the brother of my father-in-law. And that's all.

After the ceremony, we went to my mother's home and spent the afternoon there—and that was it. We rented a place to live by ourselves and—don't forget, my wife was just 17 or 18—I had to continue the same kind of work, selling and buying. It was very difficult financially, and at one point Sonia had to sleep at her mother's and I slept at mine. At first we rented a small apartment, but by 1944 things had become very difficult for us. We maintained the apartment but slept separately because we had to, financially. Not until 1948 did my wife become pregnant and we had our little girl.

But in December 1943, when we married, we confronted a terrible world. In 1944 we were well aware of the situation of Jews both in Poland and in Transnistria. We knew that millions of Jews were being killed. I knew this even before I was married. (Several years earlier, I had heard a knock at the door one night, and my mother and I went to see who was there. Standing at our door was a Jewish Polish soldier, a runaway. He by chance knocked on our door and my mother let him come in. We gave him a place to eat and sleep. It was very dangerous, and after forty-eight hours he left. This marked our awareness of the terrible circumstances for Jews in Europe.)

In 1943 and 1944, people began to talk about Auschwitz and other concentration camps, saying: "Did you hear what happened to the Hungarian Jews or Romanian Jews who were part of the West?" I did not know about Treblinka, but I heard about Auschwitz because the Hungarians were going there. We still did not grasp the magnitude of the crimes against our people.

And though we did not know about the gas chambers, we did know that Jews were being shot in forests all over Europe. This had happened to some thirty-five Jews from Bucharest.

And even as stories circulated in the beginning of 1944 from the Soviet Union, Poland, and Transnistria, we did not realize the magnitude of the crimes. We heard rumours, not details, about massacres, but we didn't know the numbers.

As 1944 progressed, the world saw the beginning of the collapse of Germany. The German army left Romania in a very orderly way. A change in government led to a more pro-Western regime. Jewish life went back to a more normal routine. It wasn't because the Antonescu government liked Jews; he just started to change his priorities because he saw that Germany was not going to be successful. As the government shifted, politicians from the forbidden political parties, including the Liberal Party, gained more power.

Still, in April 1944 Bucharest was bombed. A beautiful high building was destroyed and people were killed, including a number of well-known artists who were living in that building. We understood that it was the American army bombing our city, to threaten the remaining German army. Despite the destruction, we were happy. Finally! The war would soon end, we knew. In June, we heard about the Normandy invasion, and we knew that the Allies—we thought through Italy—would approach us. And in August 1944, the Soviet army arrived.

On August 23rd, there was another attempt in Bucharest to get rid of the Germans. The democratic parties came to power. I remember that event clearly, because Sonia and I were visiting my uncle. He had a radio, so we went to his place to hear the news, to celebrate.

Out in the street, people were singing and dancing. Oh yes! This was the end of Antonescu.

Little by little the Russians pushed west. The streets of Bucharest filled up with Russian soldiers. Indeed, my in-laws had to evacuate a room for a couple of Russian soldiers. Sonia's parents had two daughters living with them, and were very afraid that the soldiers would hurt them. I remember seeing the soldiers on the streets; they behaved quite civilized, even while trying to take off watches from your hand. I remember seeing a Russian soldier who had around ten watches on his arms. But I don't remember any significant incident.

But despite the calm, I warned myself, "I don't know if this is the beginning of the end," because we were afraid of the Communists. We experienced democracy for about six months, but when the Communists came to power I started to think about leaving Romania.

We were young and poor, and Sonia and I were each staying at our parents' apartments. I still sold whatever items I could acquire on the black market, just to be able to eat. It was still wartime, still a time of little food. Just to the west, Hungarian Jews were being deported to

Auschwitz; there were still eight more months of war. Even so, Bucharest was quieter. From time to time there were German bombs, but the Americans were chasing them. We were able to follow the news more readily on the radio and in the democratic newspapers. And the anti-Jewish laws and legislations were quietly abolished. Jewish people felt more free to go out. The Jewish community would gather at the synagogue and would talk openly about *Eretz Israel*, I was part of the Hashomer Hatzair organization, though because I was married I was more involved with work and day-to-day financial survival. I still could not find a steady job. Sonia's parents helped us, giving us food.

All in all, the Russian presence did not intrude on me the way the Germans had. I didn't feel that they particularly touched my life. I knew that there was an occupation army and that nobody liked them, but I tried to go back to study, to finish the education that I had been forced to stop. I wanted to go back to university to become an accountant. And though this was very hard and required a financial commitment, my uncle encouraged me and helped me. After a few years I earned a B.Comm degree and was able to work as an accountant.

I functioned in many languages in Romanian society. In addition to speaking Romanian, I knew Yiddish and Hebrew. I could follow German, from its similarity to Yiddish, but I hated the Germans so much that I didn't want to pronounce anything in their language. When the Russians arrived, however, I could not communicate with them. I did meet the occasional Jewish Russian soldier and was able to exchange words with him in Yiddish. Sometimes I would meet a Jewish Russian on the street or at the cinema. I'd hear them speaking Yiddish and would walk up to them to say *Shalom*.

Sonia and I tried to live a quiet, uncomplicated life. I was afraid to get involved with politics, as I was a married man with a very young daughter. I could hardly make a living so it was a very difficult time. I followed the news on the radio and in the newspapers, knowing that we could not change anything. The Soviet army was there, taking things under their control; it was not a free press. As during the Germans' time, everything was monitored and checked. Whatever they wanted us to know, we knew. There was radio but it was hard to find the European channel. I didn't have my own radio.

At the end of the summer 1944, the Russians were pushing into Germany. We had been waiting for that moment since May. Things had, happily, stabilized for us, and we were living a very quiet, uneventful life. True, food was rationed, but we were not suffering from hunger, despite shortages of flour, sugar, and bread. We remained living near our parents, on Eagle Street. It was considered a Jewish district, but we had Christian neighbours. To our right was the cobbler, and I eventually submitted his name to Yad Vashem in Jerusalem, calling him a righteous gentile. To our left was a Christian German family, with three daughters, one of whom was very close to us. The other two were pro-Nazi but we didn't have problems with them.

When the war finally was drawing to an end, with V-E Day in May 1945, we followed the news and rejoiced to know that Hitler and Mussolini were dead. There were celebrations throughout Europe, and our friends who had radios informed us of the news. Happy crowds filled the centre of Bucharest.

But it was also in that year, 1945, that we first learned the extent of the killings, and people uttered the word *Auschwitz*. There was no denial, no rumour. We knew that Jews were put in chambers, were told to get undressed for a shower. And the shower was gas. We read about this in the newspapers, and people talked about it. At first we couldn't believe it—we thought that we were hearing propaganda against Germany, but soon we realized that it was true, done by supposedly human beings.

Now that the war was over, we saw the many photographs circulating around Europe of the dead bodies. We saw the pictures in the newspapers, in the free press, after August 23, 1944. These papers arrived from outside the country, especially the French newspapers. It was from there that we learned how the Soviets had liberated Majdanek and Auschwitz.

Of course, the Russian soldiers didn't talk about it. They couldn't communicate in our language. And the few Jewish soldiers who spoke Yiddish were so weary of the war that they preferred not to talk. Other news trickled in from survivors who had run away and returned to tell what they had seen and been through. They were the actual witnesses.

I was more fortunate than many other Romanian Jews. We had never had much contact with my father's family even before the war, so we did not know if we suffered losses with them. My mother's family lived in the lower part of Romania, an area that saw fewer losses than the northern parts of the country. We were personally not affected as badly as others, and yet it was still shocking to read the newspapers and also to hear from witnesses who showed us how cruelly they themselves had been treated. With every word spoken, and every article I read, I knew that we were experiencing the disappearance of Romanian Jewry. And there were as yet no reports about the killing fields of Transnistria; I only fully grasped what had happened there when I arrived in Montreal more than a decade later.

Our family life began to unravel with the end of the war and the Communist takeover of Romania. Though we all survived—my parents and my three sisters—Sonia and I knew that we had to leave. One of the most painful moments of my life occurred when I had to depart from my parents. Our baby was on the way, and we had to choose a better life for her. On March 3, 1948, our baby Malca was born. And we knew we had to take her out of the country as soon as possible. I pleaded with my mother to come with us to Israel, but she replied, "I want to see you and your sisters leave, and then we'll talk about it." But her voyage to be with us never occurred. She passed away, probably from cancer, after I had come to Canada. My father survived for another few years and then he, too, also passed away, of old age. My three sisters arrived in Israel after me. All three of them remained there.

*　*　*

The war was over. From 1945 to 1950, we subsisted, began recovering our lives, but suffered with our memories of so many losses. I did every type of work that I could find. My uncle was the manager of the Commerce and Industry Bank, one of the great banks of Bucharest. Because of his high position, I could take on small bookkeeping and accounting jobs. I was happy to earn a living and support our small family.

We knew, instinctively, that it was time to leave Romania. Enough was enough in the graveyard of European anti-Semitism. During the war we had seen the very extremes of deportations and deaths, murderous, gruesome torture and death, all resulting from an inbred hatred of Jews. I had felt its tentacles from the time I was a little boy. I was haunted by the thought that my father had been subjected to disrespect and lack of consideration only because he was a Jew. Enough was enough. I would not pass this legacy onto my small daughter.

When Israel was granted independence in 1948, I said to myself, "I am not going to live here in Romania for the rest of my life, and I am not going to let my little daughter live in this kind of system and country." My mother was very heartbroken but she told me, "You are doing the right thing, my son."

The Israeli government had already established a procedure to apply for immigration. The process was supposed to take about a year. When we received confirmation of our acceptance, it was one of the happiest moments of my life. But there was no financial assistance, and that thought was daunting.

We left in 1950. I remember how my mother came to the station crying, and when the train started to move she ran after it. Neither of us understood that we would never see each other again.

We took the train to a port city and then boarded a ship to the port of Haifa. Then we, along with several hundred other Romanians, were sent to a tent city called Shaar Aliyah. My little daughter was two years old, and she asked, "Oh Mommy, where are the carpets?"

We lived in a tent for about six months until we found a place of our own. But my family was split up because to find work I had to go wherever the jobs led. For a while I worked in Haifa, and my wife and daughter lived in Tel Aviv with her parents. I would get home to them only on Friday night for Shabbat. It was good for Sonia that her parents, Berta and Yosef Lift, had come shortly after us. They didn't want to be in Romania for one day without us, especially because they missed our little girl. Sonia's sister Marga left Romania, too, for Israel with her parents. They all lived together while I did what I had to do. Five or six people from the family lived together in one small room. I had hoped that my parents and sister would come but my mother became ill and said that the adjustment would be too difficult for her. I was happy, though, that my three sisters did make *aliyah* and I spent many hours with them in Tel Aviv.

I also recall how moved I was to go to Jerusalem. I prayed there that I would one day again see my parents. I still remember the spiritual feeling of that city. When I write about Israel, I always feel as though I am right there, in that moment.

I was already too old to be drafted into the army. However, during the Sinai War of 1956, I served as a reservist, which made me the happiest person in the world. I learned to use a gun for the first time, and was very happy, very, very proud. What a contrast to when I had reached the age to be drafted into the Romanian army—they had rejected me. In

Sinai I did not see combat but worked as an accountant in an office, keeping records. I did not personally fight, but when I returned to civilian life, the army gave me a little token of recognition for my so-called bravery.

There were also political tensions, though I felt that we could overcome them. My family felt otherwise.

By 1959, Sonia's parents decided that they wanted to go to Canada because of the opportunities there for their daughter. They didn't want to stay in Israel—it was a land of stifling heat, unemployment, and hardship. When they left for Montreal, my wife said, "I don't want to live without my parents. I want to go with them." It was a difficult period for me but I wanted to please Sonia. I loved her and I loved our daughter Monica (Malca). It was hard for many people to resist the call to move to a more prosperous America or Canada.

It was a hard choice for me, but I believed that I could be a Zionist no matter where I lived. I had mastered Hebrew, had been a Zionist since my teenage years, and I justified moving away by thinking that I could promote the State of Israel from elsewhere, using my writing skills to tell people about our new land. I felt that I could deliver the message from anywhere, and Montreal was a good place to choose.

We did return a few times to Tel Aviv because my sisters remained there. Every time I went back, I went to Jerusalem, of course.

We came to Canada by ship, entering the country in Halifax after stopping in Italy and France. I don't remember the name of the ship. It was just the three of us traveling together, for many days. We arrived in Montreal in the summer, and my wife's sister was already established, so she helped us get settled.

I found work immediately, again as a bookkeeper. I only did office work, no physical labour. I was not particularly happy, though, as I still longed for Israel. It took me a long time to get used to Montreal and meet people and talk, even though I had no language problems. I had

Baruch and his daughter Monica (Malca) z"l, 1987

learned French back in Romania, and had learned English in Israel. It wasn't hard to integrate into Canada—it was just hard for me not to be in Israel! I didn't even mind the weather; it was similar to Romania's. In both countries winter starts in November and lasts as long as Passover. Canada in some ways even reminded me of prewar Romania: I was free to wander where I wanted.

Our Jewish life in Quebec was full, though we did experience anti-Semitism to a certain degree. It was not as aggressive as in Romania, but I still felt it. I looked around for a synagogue in which I could feel comfortable. That took a number of years of exploring different synagogues on Saturdays. But when we were established, we became members of the Chevra Shas, on Côte-des-Neiges Road. We were living on Decelles Avenue, in walking distance to the synagogue. I was a member there for many years.

People ask me how I found happiness and fulfillment. I can say that it was mainly through my wife and my daughter. Sonia is an exceptional human being; very courageous, hard working, dedicated, lovable. I was glad that Sonia did not have to take a job; I earned enough to send our daughter to school.

# Part III

Graduation, Concordia U., M.A., 1986

# My Legacy

I am now in my late nineties, weak in body but strong as ever in my intense drive to pass on my message. I moved from hellish Nazi-run Europe, to the brilliant country of Israel, and then to Canada, where I re-established my life. Now I need to sum up my goals, to pass them on not just to my grandchildren and great-grandchildren, but to all who dream of the goals of the Jewish people, and to all who fight anti-Semitism. In this spirit, I want to describe the work and projects in which I humbly participated, at the Holocaust Centre in Montreal, on a broader campaign to make the world know what happened to the Jews of Transnistria, and at the Canadian Institute for Jewish Research, where I still serve as research director.

## The Montreal Holocaust Memorial Centre

I first encountered the Montreal Holocaust Centre while I was visiting the Jewish Public Library in the 1970s. In their basement, a small room was allocated to memories of the Shoah. The photographs were startling.

I got acquainted with Krisha Starker, a survivor, a very strong, capable woman. She is the person who really gave life to this institution. She and other survivors would meet there nearly every day, committed to creating a memorial and educational resource centre. At that point in the late twentieth century, survivors were only beginning to tell their stories. Until then, silence was the dominant mode of coping with the horrors. Some of the people couldn't believe the stories we heard. My experiences in Romania had been horrific and brutal, but I had not lived through the death camps.

I devoted myself to this institution, coming there after work and never saying no to their requests. Students began to visit the centre, and I was instrumental in teaching them our history, in talks to classes and small groups. Krisha encouraged me to talk; and I was the voice of the Romanian Jews here. She said, "Come Baruch, whenever you can, come and tell your story." Little by little, the Holocaust Memorial Centre grew into the invaluable place it is today. And over time, survivors in Montreal donated items that they owned, artifacts, their yellow stars, a striped uniform from Auschwitz.

Lectures at schools, for students of all ages, proved to be very effective. In time, we expanded these talks to higher levels, and I would speak to classes at McGill and Concordia University.


*Transnistria: Telling the Unknown Story*


There is a region of Romania, a site of slaughter for hundreds of thousands, which was ignored by historians until the 1980s. Transnistria was a place of deportations, of forced labour, of mass killings. Many thousands were sent over the Dniestr River, at the border between Romania and Russia, where they were trapped and vulnerable.

As details came to light, I met with survivors from the area, and made it my mission to tell their story, to put Transistria on the map of anti-Jewish destruction. This was my major achievement. This was my evidence in the war of words that refused to admit that there had been a Holocaust in Romania.

I knew of the region's history because my younger uncle had married a woman from Bessarabia, in the eastern part of Romania, from the city of Soroka. Jews were deported to Transnistria in the early 1940s, where they were slaughtered in the cities of Dorohoi, Galaţi (Galatz), and Iaşi. I had heard rumours when I lived in Bucharest—several hundred Jews were deported, though the bulk of Jews who were sent off to Transnistria had lived in Moldova, Bessarabia, and Bukovina. Several hundred thousand Jews were taken against their will to Transnistria.

I heard the stories in Bucharest because a number of community leaders had been picked up. Because of their status as leaders or lawyers, they were sent back after a short while, and people started to learn about the conditions there. For example, I heard about the deportation and return of Dr. Wilhelm Filderman, the leader of the Jewish community. He returned and his associates spread the news through word of mouth. He also helped to block plans to deport Romanian Jews to concentration camps in Poland.

The news about Transnistria hit me hard, especially when I learned that as many as 300,000 or 400,000 Jews died there. I did not realize the full extent of Romanian complicity until the 1980s. I became so involved with the subject that people who read what I wrote about Transnistria assumed that I had been there. But for me, Transnistria symbolized the suffering of my sisters and my brothers. It was in my heart. Men, women, children, slaughtered with the complicity of the Romanian army, under the rule of the prime minister, Ion Antonescu. Their anti-Semitism was so deep that the next step, genocide, was not difficult to undertake.

Baruch Cohen with CIJR student interns, 2016

The Jews in Transnistria experienced hunger, illness, and shootings—many tried to run away, and usually that meant death. People were sent to work for twelve to fourteen hours a day. The conditions were far worse than what I experienced in the labour camp near to Bucharest.

Starting in 1944, some Jews returned to Bucharest. Among them was my uncle's wife. Also, some five thousand Jewish children arrived, and my uncle adopted a little girl, age six or seven, who now lives in Israel, where she married and raised a family. When she arrived from Transnistria, her body was full of sores and wounds; she was hungry and didn't trust anybody. Her name is Miriam, the name we gave her.

Transnistria was a human disaster. People didn't know about it. When I came to Canada I talked to people . . . I don't want to take the credit, but Transnistria was not known in Montreal.

## The Canadian Institute for Jewish Research

In 1988, I reached the age of retirement, and my thought was, "What am I going to do? I still want a full-time job." I became even more active at the Holocaust Centre, serving on committees and continuing to speak to school groups.

I also completed my bachelor's degree, and studied history with Professor Frederick Krantz at Concordia University. Professor Krantz had also established the Canadian Institute for Jewish Research, to counter anti-Israel activities on campus and to fight anti-Semitism. In 1988, I met Professor Krantz on the bus, and we started to talk. He said, "Baruch, why don't you take a Master's degree?" His inspiration led me to earn a Master's degree in Jewish philosophy. He even pushed me to go further, but I stopped at that. In the meantime, CIJR was expanding—it had started in a small room in the basement of his home, but soon moved into an office building. And I have not stopped working there, promoting solidarity with the State of Israel and exposing the world to anti-Semitism.

## Final Thoughts

Certain parts of my memory are fuzzy. But other parts recall Romania so clearly. These thoughts remain so deep in my heart and my mind. The suffering and disappointment are so profound that they still wake me from my sleep. My nightmares have never ceased, making me at times very disturbed and agitated. But I channel these feelings of despair, convinced that there is a purpose for me to go on giving testimony.

I have seen young people listening and learning, grasping what happened to the Jewish people in the twentieth century. I call them my

Baruch with Prof. Frederick Krantz and Henry Kissinger

students, even though I never was an official teacher or professor. My reward from these efforts are in the words of the letters numerous students have written to me.

I have continued my message through talking and working with students at CIJR. Gently, I remind them of my experiences, and my hope that these should serve as a warning again hatred. The focus is on Israel at CIJR, but I link events in Europe to contemporary anti-Israel events. I have come to the office every day for twenty-eight years, researching the subject of anti-Semitism, of the war against the Jews, the Holocaust. I choose articles from newspapers, organize a library, and talk to students and visitors.

There at CIJR and at the Holocaust Centre, it is my mission to see that every student will learn why the Holocaust occurred. People young and old must learn about the inhumanity of so-called humanity. Inhumanity towards other people: look what humans have done and continue to do to other humans. We should know what the other nations did to the Jews. Why were we treated that way? Because we were Jews.

Through my example, others can learn about the pains, the insults, the Jews who were beaten. I went through the streets of Romania, and was told, "You can't walk on this side, you have to go on the other side." Why? Because I was a Jew. This is what the young generation should learn and know. I survived the pains, the insults, the misery which penetrated my soul, knowing with pride that I am a Jew.

The hatred towards Judaism is not just several centuries old; it has endured for more than two thousand years. I don't think it will ever disappear. But we can fight and guard ourselves against it.

My belief is that initially human beings are good. Warm. That people want to live in peace, to create good things for the world. My message for future generations is to promote my philosophy: love thy people and thy self.

I have three great-grandchildren and I want them to know what happened. I want them to remember me not just as Baruch Cohen, but as an individual who fought for justice, who taught about the perils of anti-Jewish hatred. That he talked to you and told you what he went through. And if they have listened and can transmit this story to their own children, then my message can last forever and ever.

# A Harmonious Dream

## *poems*

# Jerusalem: City of Peace

*in honour of Professor Frederick Krantz*

O Jerusalem, shining and bright
Embraced forever with your people's love

O my people, I would sing my heart
On this night of glory
My city of love on whose
Hills my father Abraham's
Painful trial
The tears of generations of my people
Have not dared extinguish
The flames of eternal sacrifice
The flames of infinite love.
Clouds of unbearable thunder,
Lightning and endless tears
Carry me on this ever-lasting night
With endless generations' might
To you, beloved Jerusalem
Ir Shalom
City of Peace
Embraced forever with my
People's love!

# For Malca with Love

I carry the load of missing
you!
Now—I am with you
With your name—but I am
alone.

It is empty, I am left alone
the days are empty, black,
I search for your hand
Your name, no echo
the days are empty
and dark
I carry the load
within me.

*March 2003*

# *From Day to Day*

*for Malca z"l*

At times I hear your voice
from day to night
Your voice is a call
a melody

Every day I wake up
and your melody is with me . . .
Springs, summer always
with me—voices of birds
and sweet melody
Your voice, your call . . .
Don't go away,
be with me
carry me
I have you in my arms

*March 2003*

# We Need Each Other

*for Dolores and Henry*

Together
in harmony we flourish

Together
with joy and strength
We reach the stars!

Discord we overcome
forever!

Abundance glitters,
Mother Earth is one
for all!

*April 10, 2011*

# The Queen (1)

*Ten Years*

You are here . . .
always dancing . . .

A dancing queen
lightning from heaven
your smile

your secret presence
embraces
us

Years of darkness
are brightened
by your Queenly image

*February 10, 2012*

# The Queen (2)

*Ten Years*

*for Mollie and Cole*

I

You are here
always dancing

A dancing queen
with your smile
lightning from
heaven

Your secret presence
embraces us

Your hidden presence
is illuminating our cloudy life.

A decade of darkness
is brightened
by your queenly image
and dance.

## II

Your image is
laugh, joy
and dance
with laughter, happiness:
Mollie and Cole.

Their eyes, their smiles
are bringing your spirit
your joy, your secret
your goodness
the love for life
and dance

Ten years—a decade
an ocean of tears
a sea of pain.
You are here with your smile,
your secret:
the splendour of your smile:
Mollie and Cole.
You did not leave us!
Your secret is with us
and
pain is deep in our breaking hearts,
A queenly secret
taken away forever.

III

Your image, your smile
is illuminating our
dark days, nights and years . . .

You are the queen!
Your flame is burning
in our hearts!
We miss you!
Your flame will burn forever . . .

Spring, joy
my queen
has been taken away
forever . . .

The dream of courage
watchful
It knows that you know!
Mollie and Cole!

*March 2010*

# To Be Free

*"Kohelet sought to find out acceptable words,*
*and the words of truth in proper form."*
*—Kohelet 12:10*

*for Malcala*

To be free is to absorb
the whisper
of the lake

To be free is to absorb
the sound
of the falling leaf

To be free is to absorb
the growth of each
new blade of grass

To be free is to absorb
the whisper
of the forest trees

To be free is to live
the joy
of "BEING"

To be free is to absorb
the silence
of the "OTHER."

*Ste. Agathe at the Lake, October 17, 1998*

# Shattered!

*for Pinkas K.*

An empty quarrel
One or two unkind words
appear to be
a grateful blow
destroys years
of friendship
and the heart
is crying bitter
tears.
Is Life ever easy
to understand?
I am . . . eighty-eight!

*January–February 2008*

# Ode to the Hebrew Language

This language is poetry
The language of Moses, Abraham, David and
    Ben Yehuda
A brass trumpet blasting the cosmos destined to
    pour out floods of rage
Against the world's abuses and indifference.
This language, this Hebrew language destined to
    pour out a flood of rage
Against the world's indifference.
Thus, this language written with letters of fire is
    poetry!
It is a call from heaven to praise life.

*May 8, 2013*

# *Time*

*(on Kohelet)*

A time to embrace
A time to hug
A time to gain
A time to keep and love
and a time to lose . . .
and a time to cry . . .
and a time to
fall . . .
and a time to
go . . .

*February 10, 2012*

# I Know

I know
my leaves are starting to fall
The dew
is starting to dry.
As I make
my way, I am glad
to suffer the pains.
Would your love
save me from the coming end . . .
My soul
will rejoice
the end of my days
for every soul dies

*March 11, 2011*

# Night

Night.
The sky over the ocean
touching the hills.
Hills floating slowly beneath
the stars.
I could hear
the heavens' stillness,
now and again
a shooting star,
a meteor
flashed!
Night!

*January–February 2008*

# *A Call*

A ROAR: it is
truth itself
stepped among
mankind,
    right into the
    darkest

    flurry
Gray Faith
    next to me
    drink
    up

The world is
    gone
I have
    to carry
    you.

# *Happiness*

Happiness is Nothing he said
   It is an Illusion;
Everything under the Shining Sun
   That is Happiness said another;
And a third one praised
   Happiness as Love.
For Him—
   It is Bread and Salt.

Darkness is my Happiness says the Night
The sun-Serenity in rays of light;
The tree claims happiness is Air and Space
   The bird in her tiny nest;
A bee finds Happiness among blooming flowers.

The wise find Happiness in Reason
the Food in ridiculous things
The Coward is Happy in his hidings
The Hero in War and Danger

And the Writer of these lines
　　—who moves without fanfare—
Believes simply Happiness is
　　writing verse.

*October 15, 1985*

# Song of Praise

*for Sonia*

The universe is
like
a Continuous song
of praise
FOR you!
Love in its
Truest form
is
Selfless
It is
You!
It is the Song
of Songs! For you!

*March 23, 2009*

# *Malca*

How it it
possible?

So
Beautiful
How is
this
acceptable?

So
young
talented
like
a flying
butterfly

How
is this
possible?

I do not believe!

How come?
I am still
awaiting . . .

A blooming
Rose
taken away
taken afar . . .

and
I am still
awaiting . . .

*January–February 2008*

# *Psalm*

It is four-twenty
that black Sunday afternoon
when Monina
said
I want to say
goodbye and you slept away
and left a vacant
for eternity.

My pain
is a Psalm
without voice
when death's shell
arrived up on shore
and
I remain forever
speechless,

Seven hundred and
thirty nights—black
without you
Monina.

Tears are
flowing
and
numbers will
remain meaningless
it is all
black-night.

An echo
and I am embraced
by a sweet voice,
it is the third of
March
twenty-two
Adar
Tav-Shin-Tet.

Monina
a Psalm.

*March 10, 2002—at 4:20 pm*

# Jerusalem

Jerusalem, the city of
Psalms, tears and joy.
O! Jerusalem, embraced forever
With thy people's love!
O! Jerusalem, a jewel
Lingering in our hearts!

Lightning, thunder endlessly
From generation to generation—to infinity—
From Eden with tears,
Showering Your people with love.
With bliss in every soul,
A song of praise for golden Jerusalem.

I bring praise to you, Zion
And thanks forever and ever.
Because I live with eternal
Love for you!

# My Heart

*to Malca*

My heart belongs to you.
I recall, at times, your voice
Abba . . .
My soul, my soul over the mountains
and seas,
Tomorrow our hands will touch tenderness.
And run . . . Abba, Abba
My memory is poor
but my heart is with you
Forever you are with me,
You are for life with me.

# The Shofar Call of My Teens: Rosh Hashanah 5772

*in loving memory of beloved Malca z"l*

Within the little synagogue
The light is dim
The air is hushed around
The silence seems to pray:
We hear the Shofar sound!

O Shofar, tell us we need not fear,
Though long and hard the way,
O Shofar, bind us with thy holy strains
'Til each young heart shares in Israel's pain.
Like a trumpet clear,
Sound anew to the world,
Renew the strongest vow:
    To bear with pride now the name of Jew
    And across the endless years!
        T'keeoo!

# A Harmonious Dream

A harmonious ensemble
invaded the ocean's face.
The water's brilliance
joined the birds' ballad
ballet.

Up and down
the birds
sipped the ocean's mist!
. . . A dream!

# Symphony of Silence

A brilliant silence
marks the air.

I have been, throughout my life,
a collector of silence.

Suddenly,
the ocean's symphony
bursts around me
and fills the air with
unknown mirages.

I am embraced by the tremor
of Mahler's Earth symphony!
and
I thirst to be embraced
by the earth's
finite silence.

*Mazlátan, 2008*

# *Sadness*

Often,
In the stillness of love
 When sunset slips
  Quietly away,
a breeze is kissing
  the earth's soul
and covering the infinite.
 My heart—a tremor
Clings.
I understand
It is the night
of quiet loneliness.

# *Emily*

You are
a fountain
of Joy
and
Love.

*June 29, 2013. Saba and Safta*

# It Is the Night

*for Fred, a leader, a tribune, a friend*


Often,
In the stillness of night,
In the stillness of love
when sunset slips
exactly away,
a breeze is kissing
the earth's soul
and covering the infinite . . .

My heart, a tremor
clings
I understand
it is the night
of quiet loneliness
and dreams . . .

# *A Eulogy*

White on White,
Silently we wait,
As a people to their prophet,
Awaiting a final prophesy,
A prophesy of life.

Like a crystal she falls,
Every joy, every fear,
Every sorrow, every pain,
Every emotion, every moral,
Universal and Eternal.
All that was, all that shall be,
Unified in one.  In a tear.
How can we interpret your message?
Should we laugh? Should we cry?
Should we wait for our prophet,
To explain his confusing words?

Slowly the tear evaporates,
Disappearing into the air,
Surrounding us and comforting us,
We know you are a part of us.

We must go on so that we too may
leave our everlasting tear.

www.ingramcontent.com/pod-product-compliance
Lightning Source LLC
Chambersburg PA
CBHW060054100426
42742CB00014B/2826